Burning Money

THE COST OF SMOKING

Tobacco: The Deadly Drug

Burning Money

The Cost of Smoking

by
Amy N. Thomas

Burning Money: The Cost of Smoking

MASON CREST PUBLISHERS INC.
370 Reed Road
Broomall, Pennsylvania 19008
(866)MCP-BOOK (toll free)
www.masoncrest.com

First Printing

9 8 7 6 5 4 3 2 1

ISBN 978-1-4222-0242-5
ISBN 978-1-4222- 0230-2 (series)

Library of Congress Cataloging-in-Publication Data

Thomas, Amy N.
  Burning money : the cost of smoking / Amy N. Thomas.
      p. cm. — (Tobacco : the deadly drug)
  Includes bibliographical references and index.
  ISBN 978-1-4222-0242-5   ISBN 978-1-4222-1326-1
 1. Smoking—Costs—Juvenile literature. 2. Smoking—Health aspects
—Costs—Juvenile literature. 3. Smoking—Economic aspects—Juvenile
literature. I. Title.
  HV5735.T49 2009
  338.4'367973--dc22
                              2008019472

Design by MK Bassett-Harvey.
Produced by Harding House Publishing Service, Inc.
www.hardinghousepages.com
Cover design by Peter Culotta.
Printed in The United States of America.

Contents

1745

Introduction

Tobacco has been around for centuries. In fact, it played a major role in the early history of the United States. Tobacco use has fallen into and out of popularity, sometimes based on gender roles or class, or more recently, because of its effects on health. The books in the Mason Crest series TOBACCO: THE DEADLY DRUG, provide readers with a look at many aspects of tobacco use. Most important, the series takes a serious look at why smoking is such a hard habit to break, even with all of the available information about its harmful effects.

The primary ingredient in tobacco products that keeps people coming back for another cigarette is nicotine. Nicotine is a naturally occurring chemical in the tobacco plant. As plants evolved over millions of years, they developed the ability to produce chemical defenses against being eaten by animals. Nicotine is the tobacco plant's chemical defense weapon. Just as too much nicotine can make a person feel dizzy and nauseated, so the same thing happens to animals that might otherwise eat unlimited quantities of the tobacco plant.

Nicotine, in small doses, produces mildly pleasurable (rewarding) experiences, leading many people to dose themselves repeatedly throughout the day. People carefully dose themselves with nicotine to maximize the rewarding experience. These periodic hits of tobacco also help people avoid unpleasant (toxic) effects, such as dizziness, nausea, trembling, and sweating, which can occur when someone takes in an excessive amount of nicotine. These unpleasant effects are sometimes seen when a person smokes for the first time.

Although nicotine is the rewarding component of cigarettes, it is not the cause of many diseases that trouble smokers, such as lung cancer, heart attacks, and strokes. Many of the thousands of other chemicals in the cigarette are responsible for the increased risk for these diseases among smokers. In some cases, medical research has identified cancer-causing chemicals in the burning cigarette. More research is needed, because our understanding of exactly how cigarette smoking causes many forms of cancer, lung diseases (emphysema, bronchitis), heart attacks, and strokes is limited, as is our knowledge on the effects of secondhand smoke.

The problem with smoking also involves addiction. But what is addiction? Addiction refers to a pattern of behavior, lasting months to years, in which a person engages in the intense, daily use of a pleasure-producing (rewarding) activity, such as smoking. This type of use has medically and personally negative effects for the person. As an example of negative medical consequences, consider that heavy smoking (nicotine addiction) leads to heart attacks and lung cancer. As an example of negative personal consequences, consider that heavy smoking may cause a loss of friendship, because the friend can't tolerate the smoke and/or the odor.

Nicotine addiction includes tolerance and withdrawal. New smokers typically start with fewer than five cigarettes per day. Gradually, as the body becomes adapted to the presence of nicotine, greater amounts are required to obtain the same rewarding effects, and the person eventually smokes fifteen to twenty or more cigarettes per day. This is tolerance, meaning that more drug is needed to achieve the same rewarding effects. The brain becomes "wired" differently after long-term exposure to nicotine, allowing the brain to tolerate levels of nicotine that would otherwise be toxic and cause nausea, vomiting, dizziness and anxiety.

When a heavy smoker abruptly stops smoking, irritability, headache, sleeplessness, anxiety, and difficulty concentrating all develop within half a day and trouble the smoker for one to two weeks. These withdrawal effects are generally the opposite of those produced by the drug. They are another external sign that the brain has become wired differently because of long-term exposure to nicotine. The withdrawal effects described above are accompanied by craving. For the nicotine addict, craving is a state of mind in which having a cigarette seems the most important thing in life at the moment. For the nicotine addict, craving is a powerful urge to smoke.

Nicotine addiction, then, can be understood as heavy, daily use over months to years (with tolerance and withdrawal), despite negative consequences. Now that we have definitions of *nicotine* and *addiction*, why read the books in this series? The answer is simple: tobacco is available everywhere to persons of all ages. The books in the series TOBACCO: THE DEADLY DRUG are about understanding the beginnings, natural history, and consequences of nicotine addiction. If a teenager smokes at least one cigarette daily for a month, that person has an 80 percent chance of becoming a lifetime, nicotine-addicted, daily smoker, with all the negative consequences.

But the series is not limited to those topics. What are the characteristic beginnings of nicotine addiction? Nicotine addiction typically begins between the ages of twelve and twenty, when most young people decide to try a first cigarette. Because cigarettes are available everywhere in our society, with little restriction on purchase, nearly everyone is faced with the decision to take a puff from that first cigarette. Whether this first puff leads to a lifetime of nicotine addiction depends on several factors. Perhaps the most important factor is DNA (genetics), as twin studies tell us that most of the risk for nicotine addiction is genetic, but there is a large role for nongenetic factors (environment), such as the smoking habits of friends. Research is needed to identify the specific genetic and environmental factors that shape a person's decision to continue to smoke after that first cigarette. Books in the series also address how peer pressure and biology affect one's likelihood of smoking and possibly becoming addicted.

It is difficult to underestimate the power of nicotine addiction. It causes smokers to continue to smoke despite life-threatening events. When heavy smokers have a heart attack, a life-threatening event often directly related to smoking, they spend a week or more in the hospital where they cannot smoke. So they are discharged after enforced abstinence. Even though they realize that smoking contributed strongly to the heart attack, half of them return to their former smoking habits within three weeks of leaving the hospital. This decision to return to smoking increases the risk of a second heart attack. Nicotine addiction can influence powerfully the choices we make, often prompting us to make choices that put us at risk.

TOBACCO: THE DEADLY DRUG doesn't stop with the whys and the hows of smoking and addiction. The series includes books that provide readers with tools they can use to not take that first cigarette, how they can stand up to negative peer pressure, and know when they are being unfairly influenced by the media. And if they do become smokers, books in the series provide information about how they can stop.

If nicotine addiction can be a powerful negative effect, then giving people information that might help them decide to avoid—or stop—smoking makes sense. That is what TOBACCO: THE DEADLY DRUG is all about.

— *Wade Berrettini MD, PhD*

CHAPTER

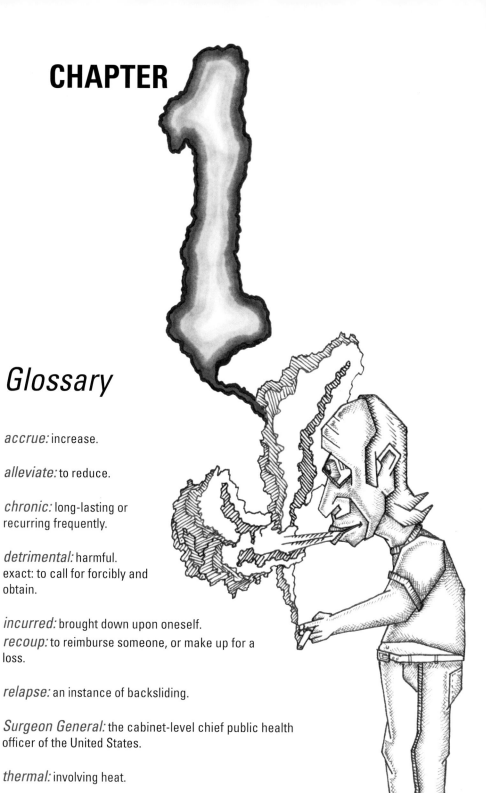

Glossary

accrue: increase.

alleviate: to reduce.

chronic: long-lasting or recurring frequently.

detrimental: harmful.
exact: to call for forcibly and obtain.

incurred: brought down upon oneself.
recoup: to reimburse someone, or make up for a loss.

relapse: an instance of backsliding.

Surgeon General: the cabinet-level chief public health officer of the United States.

thermal: involving heat.

The Cost of Smoking

Smoking a single cigarette recently turned deadly in a small Western town. Twelve days later, the local newspaper ran the following article:

> The cause of a Dec. 29 apartment fire . . . that resulted in the death of one high school senior and serious injuries to another was ruled accidental and was likely caused by unextinguished smoking materials in the living room, according to [the fire and rescue chief].
>
> Cigarettes, lighters and candles were found at the scene and could have been the cause of the fire.

When the smoker lit up a cigarette, he didn't intend to set a fire, burn down an apartment building, or cause injuries and death. He was just doing something he'd probably done many times before. But this time was different; this time the act of smoking *incurred* a significant unexpected cost.

A list of the pros and cons of smoking would make something immediately evident: The list of pros would be either nonexistent or very, very short. The list of cons, however, would be extensive because smoking has many *detrimental* effects. University and government reports in recent years have shed light on both well-known and hidden costs of smoking. This book takes a hard look at some of those costs, dividing them into the prices paid by individuals who develop a smoking habit and the costs levied against our society as a whole. Chapter 1 briefly examines the four major cost categories: 1.) accidental fires, 2.) cigarette-induced illnesses, 3.) quitting and prevention, and 4.) purchase and production. The remaining chapters delve more deeply into each of these subjects.

Besides the obvious cost of purchasing the tobacco product, the smoker incurs many personal health and safety costs. But it's not just the individual smoker who pays a price for his cigarette habit; his family and the larger community also bear a share of the cost. About 20 percent of North Americans smoked in 2007, but all members of society pay a price. Society as a whole suffers health and safety consequences and bears a financial burden brought on by cigarette smoking.

Accidental Fires

Some costs, such as buying a pack of cigarettes, fall neatly under the personal-cost label. Others, such as the impact of a tragedy, *extract* both a personal toll and a cost to society. Although smoking cigarettes results in a

Smoking can result in many harmful consequences, both for those who smoke and for the people around them. For example, carelessness while smoking is a common cause of building fires.

number of costs, the most catastrophic may be those caused by smoking-related fires. Cigarette-related fires across the country range from minor mishaps at home where burning ash falls on a sofa or shirt, to major building fires that destroy several homes or other structures. Minor accidents result in cleanup and replacement costs. Major fires can cause injuries that require hospitalization in addition to their larger cleanup and rebuilding costs.

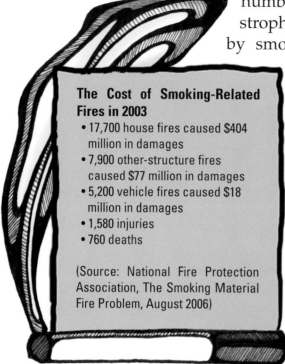

The Cost of Smoking-Related Fires in 2003
- 17,700 house fires caused $404 million in damages
- 7,900 other-structure fires caused $77 million in damages
- 5,200 vehicle fires caused $18 million in damages
- 1,580 injuries
- 760 deaths

(Source: National Fire Protection Association, The Smoking Material Fire Problem, August 2006)

Personal Costs

Those responsible for cigarette-related fires, those who are in the immediate vicinity, and those who own buildings involved in the blaze pay the price in property damage, injuries, and even death.

The two teens in the apartment fire described at the beginning of this chapter were among the thousands of people who arrived at hospital emergency rooms due to smoking-related accidents that year. According to a report by the National Fire Protection Association (NFPA), tobacco products caused 10,000 emergency-room visits in 2006. These visits included poisonings from ingesting tobacco products and *thermal* burns from cigarette-caused fires. About 700 people died from smoking-related fires.

Societal Costs

The NFPA found that smoking-related fires greatly affected people other than the smoker. The report wrote, "The same special study of well-documented fatal home smoking-material fires found that one fatal victim in four (24%) is *not* the smoker whose cigarette started the fire."

Families and communities also pay the cost for operating fire departments. While communities of a certain size must build and staff fire departments, regardless of

Smoking-caused fires can affect more than the person who was smoking; family members, as well as the entire community, suffer the consequences as well.

whether cigarette-induced fires occur, fires caused by cigarettes increase the operating costs of those departments and may cause injuries to firefighters. Additionally, insurance premiums may increase for everyone when companies try to *recoup* the money they pay out because of smoking-related fires.

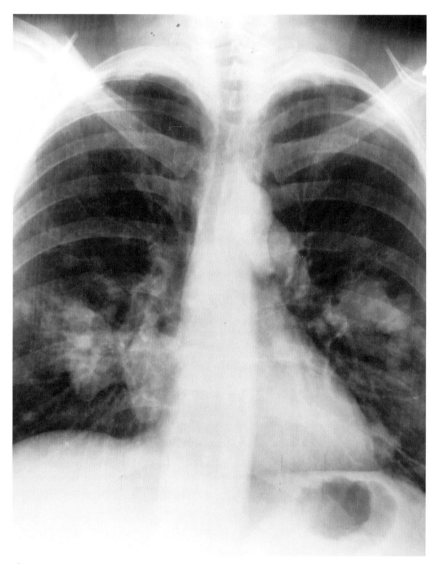

Smoking cigarettes can lead to lung problems. The spots on the lungs shown in this x-ray are possible cancerous growths caused by smoking.

Cigarette-induced fires often lead to immediate injuries and death. Long-term health concerns, on the other hand, are a common consequence of *chronic* cigarette use.

Cigarette-Induced Illnesses

For more than seventy years, researchers have understood that smoking cigarettes causes heart disease and lung cancer. Tobacco researcher Larry C. White discovered that medical professionals knew as early as 1938 that smoking shortened the expected adult life span. That's when Johns Hopkins professor Raymond Pearl reported his findings on this subject to the New York Academy of Medicine. White noted that the groundbreaking story about Pearl's findings ran not on the front page but in the back pages of the *New York Times*.

Personal Costs

"Each year, an estimated 438,000 Americans die as a result of smoking or exposure to second-hand smoke, and for each person who dies from a smoking-related disease, about 20 more are living with a smoking-attributable illness," reported the Centers for Disease Control and Prevention (CDC) in their 2006 state data on smoking.

Cancer Deaths Caused by Smoking
- 88 percent of lung cancer deaths in men
- 83 percent of larynx (voice box) cancer deaths in men
- 72 percent of cancer of the esophagus deaths in men
- 71 percent of lung cancer deaths in women
- 75 percent of larynx (voice box) cancer deaths in women
- 55 percent of cancer of the esophagus deaths in women

(Source: American Cancer Society Survey, 2006)

Twenty-two percent of current smokers are high school students. The 2004 report from the *Surgeon General* concluded that each day more than four thousand young people smoke their first cigarette. The Surgeon General's Report concluded that the decision to smoke directly affects personal health in the following ways:

- Smoking causes cancers of the mouth, throat, larynx (voice box), lung, esophagus, pancreas, kidney, and bladder.
- Smoking causes cancers of the stomach and the cervix, and acute myeloid leukemia, which is a cancer of the blood.

Many smokers start when they are teenagers; more than 4,000 young people start smoking every day.

- Cigarette smoking causes most cases of lung cancer.
- Smoking causes cardiovascular (heart and blood vessel) diseases including high blood pressure, hardening of the arteries, coronary heart disease, stroke, and congestive heart failure.
- Smoking causes reduced fetal growth and low birth weight.

Societal Costs

Heart disease, lung cancer, and other smoking-related diseases affect individuals, but these illnesses also impact the broader society. Family members spend time caring for those who are ill. Coworkers shoulder extra work duties and employers spend money hiring temporary staff to fill positions left vacant when workers are absent for extended periods due to illness and treatment. Additionally, health insurance premiums increase for everyone when companies try to recover money paid to doctors, pharmacies, and hospitals for smoking-related treatments.

Society must also contend with secondhand smoke and the health problems it generates. "More than 126 million nonsmoking Americans, including children and adults, are regularly exposed to secondhand smoke," concluded the CDC in 2007. The CDC reported that

The Cost of Cigarette-Induced Illness per Year
Direct medical costs: $75 billion
Lost productivity costs: $92 billion
Total: $167 billion in annual health-related economic losses

(Source: Centers for Disease Control and Prevention, "Targeting Tobacco Use: The Nation's Leading Cause of Preventable Death," 2007)

of those exposed to secondhand smoke, "an estimated 3,000 nonsmoking Americans die of lung cancer, more than 35,000 die of heart disease, and about 150,000 to 300,000 children younger than 18 months have lower respiratory tract infections."

Two paths reduce a person's risk for long-term smoking-related illness: quitting smoking or, better yet, not starting in the first place.

Quitting and Prevention

"Within 20 minutes after you smoke that last cigarette, your body begins a series of changes that continue for years," according to the U.S. Surgeon General. The health benefits within three months of quitting include a drop in heart rate, removal of carbon monoxide from the blood, and improved lung function.

The CDC conducted National Health Interview Surveys over a number of years. According to their 2007 updated information, the number of smokers declined from 42 percent in 1965 to 20 percent in 2004. During that same period, the number of former smokers grew from 13 percent to 21 percent.

Personal Costs

Quitting smoking takes time. The CDC reported in 2007: "Quitting tobacco use is difficult and may require multiple attempts, as users often *relapse* because of withdrawal symptoms." To help

Teen Smokers Want to Quit
More than 54 percent of high school–aged cigarette smokers in the United States tried to quit smoking within the preceding year.

(Source: Centers for Disease Control and Prevention Fact Sheet, March 2007)

smokers who want to quit, the CDC's National Tobacco Control Program established a national free counseling program. People can call the national quitline, 1-800-QUIT-NOW, and receive assistance and information about local smoking-cessation resources.

In addition to counseling, those who want to quit can purchase nicotine-replacement therapies. In 2000, the Food and Drug Administration approved six medications to help smokers quit. Five of them reduce withdrawal symptoms by providing nicotine to the body. The sixth is not a form of nicotine replacement. Instead, it blocks signals to the brain that cause the urge to smoke.

Quitting cigarettes can be extremely hard. However, it can be done through a combination of counseling and nicotine replacement therapy.

Many public places now are smoke free in an attempt to reduce the negative
health effects on the public due to secondhand smoke.

Societal Costs

In 2007, the CDC urged employers to provide smoking-cessation programs as an employee benefit. The report said, *"Paying for tobacco use cessation treatments is the single most cost-effective health insurance benefit for adults that can be provided to employees."* The CDC concluded that the benefits of paying for smoking cessation outweighed the cost. According to the report, "It costs between 10 and 40 cents per member per month to provide a comprehensive tobacco cessation benefit. . . . In contrast, the annual cost of tobacco use is about $3,400 per smoker or about $7.18 for each pack of cigarettes sold."

Society also pays for tobacco-prevention programs. Much of the money used for such programs comes from the multibillion-dollar Master Settlement Agreement made between tobacco companies, forty-six states, and Puerto Rico, the U.S. Virgin Islands, American Samoa, Guam, the Northern Mariana Islands, and the District of Columbia. Money also comes from cigarette taxes.

In addition to smoking itself, society is concerned about secondhand smoke. In an effort to cut down on smoke exposure, many communities established non-smoking government offices and smoke-free restaurants and other public spaces, which has led to cleaner air in those environments.

When individuals continue to take up the smoking habit and refuse (or are unable) to quit, the costs of purchase and production continue to *accrue*.

Purchase and Production

The U.S. Department of Agriculture (USDA) reports that consumers spent $84 billion on cigarettes in 2006. In addition to cigarettes, many smokers purchased gum, mints, and dry cleaning to *alleviate* the smell of smoke.

Personal Costs

According to a 2006 National Institute on Drug Abuse survey, the average smoker buys 265 packs of cigarettes each year, spending $1,129 annually. Massachusetts *SouthCoast Today* writer Vivian Marino wrote, "Marcy Balk figures she could have bought a new car or taken her husband and two children on a luxury vacation had she saved and invested all the money spent over two decades on cigarettes."

Balk told Marino in a 1997 interview, "I never really sat down and did the numbers [but] . . . I smoked one and a half packs a day for 22 years. I also probably dry-cleaned twice the rate as I do now." Marino noted that Balk "conservatively estimates losses around $15,000, not including the money spent trying to kick her habit through acupuncture and other methods."

Although those who smoke incur great costs to their personal budgets, society pays an even greater price.

Societal Costs

Who Smokes?
Approximately 22.8 percent of the American population smokes—25.2 percent of men and 20.7 percent of women.

(Source: American Lung Association)

According to USDA statistics, in 2006, the United States grew enough tobacco to manufacture 484 billion cigarettes. The process used to make all those cigarettes generates hazardous waste. According to tobacco researcher Thomas E. Novotny,

The tobacco manufacturing process produces liquid, solid, and airborne waste. Among those wastes, some

Litter from cigarette butts and other smoking materials is unsightly and leads to environmental degradation as well.

The pesticides used to grow tobacco crops can run off into water supplies,
causing water pollution.

materials, including nicotine, are designated by the EPA as Toxics Release Inventory (TRI) chemicals.

Cigarettes were also responsible for 29 percent of litter collected in the 2005 International Coastal Cleanup (ICC). According to the ICC, volunteers collected 8.2 million pounds (3.7 million kilograms) of debris. Cigarette trash comprised approximately 2.4 million pounds (1.1 million kg) of the total debris collected.

Other Costs

All costs of smoking do not fall neatly under the four categories discussed in this book. One is the unpleasant residual odor of smoked cigarettes. This registers as a personal cost levied against homeowners and automobile owners who smoke, and against their families.

Smoke Odors

Odors from cigarette smoke can be tough to live with and reduce the resale value of smokers' homes. *Washington Post* staff writer Dina ElBoghdady reported the negative effect of smoke odors in a June 2007 story:

> Olga Lukianova loved the location, the look and the price of the cute bungalow she and her husband spotted while shopping for a new home—until she swung the front door open.
> "The place just reeked of cigarette smoke," said Lukianova, 31, a Capitol Hill resident and a scientist by training. "We could smell it before we stepped in. At the time, we were both smokers, and it even bugged us. . . . It was gross."
> Even though they said the house was "awesome" in every other way, the couple fretted about

whether they could get rid of the stench and, if so, at what cost. The smoke had seeped into the furniture, the textured wallpaper, the carpeting and even the wood rail of the staircase. They concluded that the financial—and emotional—drain of dealing with the odor would not be worth it.

According to the National Association of Realtors (NAR), a clean, odor-free home sells faster and at a higher price than a home that is messy or has odors. The organization says sellers can reduce smoke odor by removing carpets and getting rid of upholstered furniture. The NAR notes, "Cleanup can involve scrubbing all walls and ductwork, repainting everything, and replacing carpets." In homes subjected to heavy smoking, the

Trying to sell a car that smells like cigarette smoke can be difficult; cars owned by smokers can sell for up to ten percent less than cars that don't smell like smoke.

drastic step of drywall replacement may eliminate the odor.

Cigarette smoke also lowers the resale value of vehicles. "Consumers just love that new car smell," Joni Grey, consumer-advice editor for *Kelley Blue Book*, said in a 2007 SmartMoney.com interview. She added that automobiles owned by smokers are more difficult to sell and generally sell for 10 percent less than cars previously owned by nonsmokers.

Cost to Eliminate Home Smoke Odors
For an average family:

- $290 to dry-clean clothing
- $1,500 to $3,000 to wash walls, windows, and floors
- $5,000 for carpet replacement
- $600 to $1,200 to install an air cleaner

(Sources: Bureau of Labor Statistics, bobvila.com, homeenergy.org, and buyerzone.com)

When it comes to the cost of smoking, though, an annoying odor is really the least of the problems.

CHATPER

Glossary

building standards and codes: rules established by government authorities regulating materials and techniques used in construction.

fixed costs: costs that are not subject to change.

gross domestic product: the total value of all goods and services produced within a country in a year, minus net income from investments in other countries.

nominal: minimal; representing a very little cost when compared with actual value received.

The Cost of Accidental Fires

Each year, smoking causes thousands of fires in the United States and around the world. These three examples illustrate the wide range of consequences.

One morning while getting ready for work, Rena sat down to smoke a cigarette and drink her morning cup of coffee. She had just showered and was wearing a fuzzy flannel robe. Her freshly washed and dried hair was coated with hairspray. As she had for thirty years, Rena shook a cigarette out of the package, placed it between her lips, and flicked a lighter.

Flames licked the end of the cigarette, and one deep draw lit the tobacco. As she pulled the cigarette from her lips and released the first puff of smoke, a bit of hot ash fell from the tip of the cigarette.

The ash landed on Rena's lap and set her robe on fire. Almost immediately, a fireball of flames engulfed her body from her knees to her neck. Next, her hair caught on fire and burned from the nape of her neck to the top of her head.

"It was over as quick as it started," recalled Rena. "And there I stood, naked and bald." Rena called her employer to request a sick day. Although Rena escaped serious burns, she purchased a wig before returning to work.

In November 2004, smoking materials ignited a deadly fire in North Carolina, according to a report by Kenneth J. Tremblay of the National Fire Protection Association (NFPA):

How Hot Is a Lit Cigarette?
- 1,292º Fahrenheit (700º Celsius) at the end of a lit cigarette as the smoker inhales
- 1,112º F (600º C) between draws in the middle of the tip
- 752º F (400º C) between draws on the tip's edges

(Sources: University of Southern California and PhysLink.com)

Although smoke from a fire in a rear bedroom of a manufactured home activated the structure's smoke alarms, two intoxicated 16-year-olds were unable to escape and died in the blaze.

Lit cigarettes can reach temperatures of almost 2,000 degrees Fahrenheit,
making it easy to ignite dangerous and deadly fires through carelessness.

Improperly extinguished cigarettes or matches can smolder and eventually
ignite, leading to life-threatening fires.

The wood- and steel-frame manufactured home, which was 86 feet (26 meters) long and 26 feet (7 meters) wide, had a wooden roof covered with asphalt shingles. Operational smoke alarms had been installed in the hallways near the bedrooms. There were no sprinklers.

The sleeping occupants first awoke to the sound of a crying and coughing baby, then realized the house was on fire. Everyone but the two teenagers escaped to a neighbor's house and called 911 at 6 a.m.

Investigators found an ashtray on a bedroom chair and noted burn patterns indicating that the fire started in that area. They determined that smoking materials ignited the chair and paper items located nearby.

The home, valued at $100,000, and its contents, valued at $50,000, were completely destroyed.

Every death, even a single injury, caused by fire represents a tragedy, but when a fire results in hundreds of injuries and deaths, that tragedy is compounded. On May 10, 2007, the Thai Labour Campaign ran an editorial in the *Bangkok Post* that read in part:

It is the anniversary of the disastrous Kader toy factory fire in Nakhon Pathom, in which 188 workers died and 469 were injured. Many of those who perished on May 10, 1993, were young women from impoverished rural families who were employed to make dolls for export. A large number of the injured suffered serious and permanent disabilities after they were forced to jump from second, third and fourth floors of the factory buildings to avoid being burned alive.

Fires can cause total destruction of a building, as was the case in the Kader toy factory fire in Nakhon Pathom.

Hundreds of workers were packed into each of the three buildings that collapsed. There were no fire extinguishers, no alarms, no sprinkler systems, and the elevated walkways between the buildings were either locked or used as storage areas. The buildings themselves were firetraps, constructed from uninsulated steel girders that buckled and gave way in less than 15 minutes. Those who attempted to flee through the narrow ground floor exits found them jammed shut. There was no escape. Afterwards the politicians in power set up committees and promised tougher safety measures to ensure that such a catastrophe could never happen again.

The promised safety measures and tighter controls were not in place . . . a full decade after the doll-factory fire . . . a court finally acquitted 14 Kader executives including the managing director, chief engineer and a major shareholder, and pinned the blame on a young Kader worker who had tossed away a cigarette butt, sending him to jail.

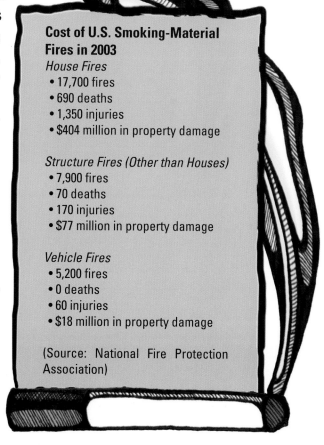

Cost of U.S. Smoking-Material Fires in 2003

House Fires
- 17,700 fires
- 690 deaths
- 1,350 injuries
- $404 million in property damage

Structure Fires (Other than Houses)
- 7,900 fires
- 70 deaths
- 170 injuries
- $77 million in property damage

Vehicle Fires
- 5,200 fires
- 0 deaths
- 60 injuries
- $18 million in property damage

(Source: National Fire Protection Association)

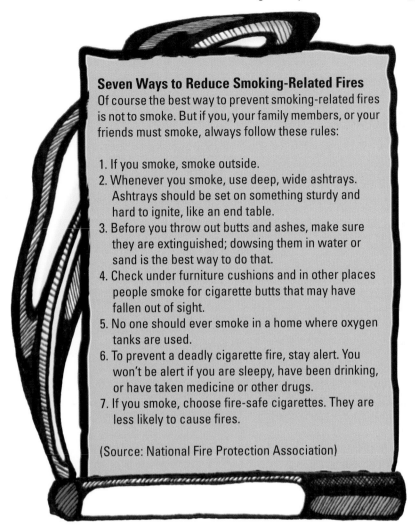

Seven Ways to Reduce Smoking-Related Fires
Of course the best way to prevent smoking-related fires is not to smoke. But if you, your family members, or your friends must smoke, always follow these rules:

1. If you smoke, smoke outside.
2. Whenever you smoke, use deep, wide ashtrays. Ashtrays should be set on something sturdy and hard to ignite, like an end table.
3. Before you throw out butts and ashes, make sure they are extinguished; dowsing them in water or sand is the best way to do that.
4. Check under furniture cushions and in other places people smoke for cigarette butts that may have fallen out of sight.
5. No one should ever smoke in a home where oxygen tanks are used.
6. To prevent a deadly cigarette fire, stay alert. You won't be alert if you are sleepy, have been drinking, or have taken medicine or other drugs.
7. If you smoke, choose fire-safe cigarettes. They are less likely to cause fires.

(Source: National Fire Protection Association)

Each year, smoking-related fires worldwide cause billions of dollars in damage to homes and businesses, as well as needless tragic deaths.

Personal Costs

In addition to injuries and deaths, the personal costs of fires started by smoking also include higher insurance premiums and, for those without insurance or under-

insured, the cost to repair and rebuild damaged structures.

Injuries and Deaths

The National Electronic Injury Surveillance System
(NEISS), maintained by the U.S. Consumer Product
Safety Commission (CPSC), compiled statistics showing
that the average number of emergency-room visits per
year due to tobacco products, for the years 2000 to 2004,
was 11,700. Roughly half those injuries were thermal
burns. One-fifth of the injuries were caused by tobacco
poisoning, presumably from swallowing tobacco. Most
of these poisonings involved children four years old or
younger. According to NFPA statistics, ten thousand

There are about 11,700 annual emergency room visits due to tobacco products.
More than half of these are caused by thermal burns.

emergency-room visits in 2004 were due to lighted tobacco products.

For more than a century, the NFPA has worked to increase fire safety around the world through the establishment of *building standards and codes* aimed at minimizing fires and fire damage. NFPA research shows that smoking materials, including cigarettes, cause about

Mattresses are extremely flammable and are easily ignited if an ash from a cigarette falls on them.

one in every four fire deaths in the United States, the most fire deaths from a single cause. The NFPA reports, "The most common material[s] first ignited in home smoking-material fire deaths were mattresses and bedding, upholstered furniture, and floor covering[s]." Contrary to popular belief, more fatal fires begin in living rooms, family rooms, and dens than in bedrooms. Falling asleep with a lit cigarette accounted for more than half the house fires caused by smoking, and drug or alcohol impairment was a factor in one-third.

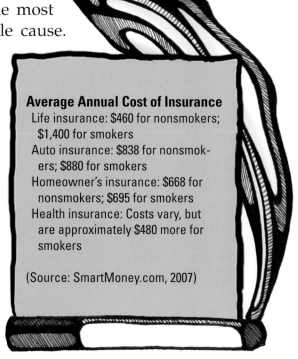

Average Annual Cost of Insurance
Life insurance: $460 for nonsmokers; $1,400 for smokers
Auto insurance: $838 for nonsmokers; $880 for smokers
Homeowner's insurance: $668 for nonsmokers; $695 for smokers
Health insurance: Costs vary, but are approximately $480 more for smokers

(Source: SmartMoney.com, 2007)

Children play a significant role in cigarette-related fires. According to research findings published in 2000 by the University of California, Davis (UC–Davis), children under the age of ten with access to cigarette lighters and matches cause 100,000 fires each year. Four hundred children die annually from fires. Put another way, children playing with lighters and matches cause 5 percent of cigarette-related fires, yet they make up 8 percent of all fire deaths each year. A 2001 U.S. Fire Administration report concludes:

> Children playing with fires are the leading cause of child fire casualties. The younger the child, the

more likely child play was involved in the start of the fire. In short, when children play with fire, they tend to hurt or kill themselves.

Insurance Costs

Smoking-related fires in the United States cause millions of dollars in damage each year. This has resulted in an increase in insurance premiums for everyone, but smokers pay even more than nonsmokers. In 2007, Smart-Money.com reporter Kelli B. Grant calculated the extra insurance costs for smokers at nearly $1,500 per year more than the costs for those who do not smoke.

Repairs and Rebuilding

Not all smoking-related fires cause large-scale disasters, such as the one cited earlier at the Kader factory in Thailand. Minor burns frequently occur when a cigarette touches a sweater, drops onto the seat of a car, or falls onto the carpet. A characteristic brown circle is often the only telltale sign of the burn. Many damaged items can be replaced or repaired at a *nominal* cost. Turning over a sofa cushion may hide the imperfection of a cushion burn. For more expensive items, such as car-

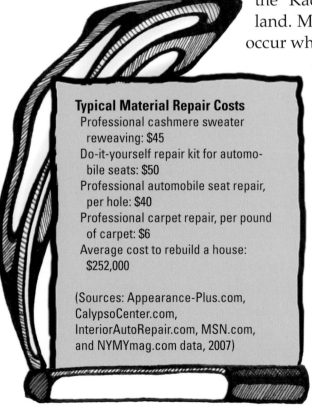

Typical Material Repair Costs
Professional cashmere sweater reweaving: $45
Do-it-yourself repair kit for automobile seats: $50
Professional automobile seat repair, per hole: $40
Professional carpet repair, per pound of carpet: $6
Average cost to rebuild a house: $252,000

(Sources: Appearance-Plus.com, CalypsoCenter.com, InteriorAutoRepair.com, MSN.com, and NYMYmag.com data, 2007)

pets and car seats, repair bills are higher.

Fire damage to homes incurs greater costs. In a 2004 article, MSN.com reporter Liz Pulliam Weston interviewed Gopal Ahluwalia, an economist for the National Association of Home Builders, about home rebuilding costs. "The average cost for building a home nationally ranges from $65 to $150 a square foot," Ahluwalia said, "with homes on the coasts and in major metropolitan areas coming in on the high end of that range." In 2006, National Public Radio reported, "The average American house size has more than doubled since the 1950s; it now stands at 2,349 square feet." Therefore, the cost to rebuild an average home destroyed by a fire would be between $150,000 and $350,000.

Individuals face great costs due to smoking-related fires, but the cost to society is even higher.

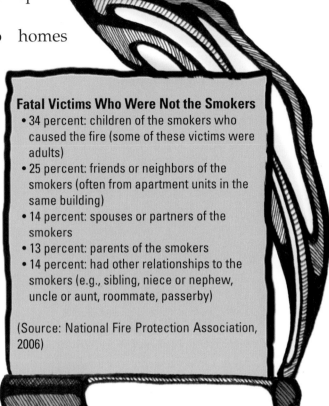

Fatal Victims Who Were Not the Smokers

- 34 percent: children of the smokers who caused the fire (some of these victims were adults)
- 25 percent: friends or neighbors of the smokers (often from apartment units in the same building)
- 14 percent: spouses or partners of the smokers
- 13 percent: parents of the smokers
- 14 percent: had other relationships to the smokers (e.g., sibling, niece or nephew, uncle or aunt, roommate, passerby)

(Source: National Fire Protection Association, 2006)

Societal Costs

Communities suffer when citizens die or are injured in accidental fires. Communities also assume the financial burden for fire departments. This involves purchasing property and equipment, building structures, hiring and training personnel, and paying all costs associated with their employment, including insurance and retirement benefits. While some of these are *fixed costs*, others increase because of smoking-caused fires.

When you add up expenses across the world, smoking-related fires cost communities billions of dollars and thousands of lives.

Innocent Victims

According to a 2006 NFPA report, one out of four fatalities caused by smoking materials is not the death of the smoker whose smoking materials started the fire. Victims are primarily the smoker's children, neighbors, and friends. Fewer than 14 percent are strangers.

Fire Departments

NFPA statistics from 2004 highlight the annual economic costs of fighting all types of fires, including those started by smoking materials. Amounts range from the cost of fire departments, at about $28 billion, to the cost of volunteer firefighters, estimated at $52 billion to $99 billion. "Therefore, the complete total cost of fire is estimated at $231–278 billion, or roughly 2 to 2.5% of U.S. *gross domestic product*," concluded the NFPA.

Just as the United States suffers tangible losses

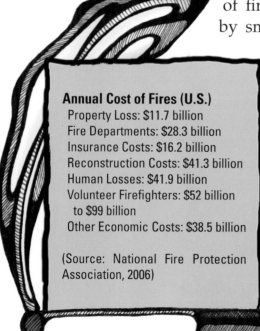

Annual Cost of Fires (U.S.)
Property Loss: $11.7 billion
Fire Departments: $28.3 billion
Insurance Costs: $16.2 billion
Reconstruction Costs: $41.3 billion
Human Losses: $41.9 billion
Volunteer Firefighters: $52 billion
   to $99 billion
Other Economic Costs: $38.5 billion

(Source: National Fire Protection Association, 2006)

Smoking-caused fires have more consequences than are at first apparent. One of these is the huge economic cost that goes into funding fire departments and volunteer firefighters.

each year from smoking-related fires, so does the global community.

Global Disasters

The production, consumption, and disposal of cigarettes burden the environment with multiple fire-related accidents and global fire disasters. The cost burden includes property destruction, hospitalization, injuries, and death.

Researchers at UC–Davis studied the impact of cigarette-related fires around the world. They gathered statistics for a ten-year period and concluded that, "Smoking is the leading cause of residential or total fire death in all eight countries with available statistics." The researchers estimate that worldwide, each year more than 1 million

In 1911, the Triangle Shirtwaist Factory in New York City ignited. More than 140 people were killed in the disaster.

fires, 28,000 injuries, and 3,300 deaths occur as a result of cigarette lighters and matches, at a cost of more than $27 billion. For most countries, the cost of these fires represents 1 percent of their entire gross domestic product. In the United States, the total is between 1 percent and 2 percent of the gross domestic product.

The 2006 NFPA study cited the percentage of smokers in countries around the world. Countries with the greater smoking-related disasters often had high percentages of smokers. Cigarette smoking accounted for sixteen major worldwide fire-related disasters in the last century, resulting in hundreds of deaths, thousands of injuries, and more than $11 billion in property loss and reconstruction costs. These disasters included the 1999 fire in the Mont Blanc Tunnel between France and Italy, which caused thirty-nine deaths and $800 million in economic losses; a 1996 incident in the Ukraine in which a lit cigarette sparked a wildfire that destroyed villages that had been evacuated after the 1986 meltdown at the Chernobyl nuclear power plant; and the 1911 Triangle Shirtwaist Factory fire in New York City, which killed 146 people.

Clearly, smoking-related fires lead to immediate negative consequences. Long-term problems also arise from cigarette use. Among them are the costs associated with cigarette-induced illnesses.

CHAPTER

Glossary

attrition: the gradual reduction of a membership or workforce.

bypass surgery: an operation to redirect blood flow through a grafted blood vessel that replaces a blocked vessel.

carcinogen: a substance that causes cancer.

periodontal: relating to tissues that surround the necks and root of a tooth.

vascular: relating to fluid-carrying vessels.

The Cost of Smoking-Induced Illness

Whether cigarette use causes illness was a source of debate for decades, but today the dangers of habitual smoking are well known. Yet even at the beginning of the twenty-first century, some dangers of smoking might surprise you. Here are three examples:

- *Seattle Times* staff reporter Stuart Eskenazi wrote about the dangers of cigarette smoke in 2005. Part of his news story reported on the dangers of cigarette smoke to a pregnant woman:

  Trish Kump enjoyed working behind the bar at the Tides Tavern in Gig Harbor, pouring drinks in front of a lineup of ashtrays—and the smoking customers who used them.

An air purifier helped suck up some of the errant smoke, but not all of it. Newly pregnant, Kump began thinking about a story told to her by a pregnant co-worker at the Tides: After her first visit to her obstetrician, the doctor was convinced that Kump's co-worker was a smoker, when in fact she had never touched a cigarette in her life.

Annual Deaths Attributed to Cigarette Smoking in the United States, 1997–2001
Lung cancer: 123,800
Other cancers: 34,700
Chronic lung disease: 90,600
Coronary heart disease: 86,800
Stroke: 17,400
Other diagnoses: 84,600

(Source: Centers for Disease Control and Prevention)

Kump began eyeing those ashtrays more perilously, concerned about her exposure to secondhand smoke and the consequences to her health and that of her unborn child.

"It's not like I could just walk away from the smoke," Kump said. "The bar, where most people smoke, was my designated area to work."

Doctors routinely warn expectant mothers about the dangers of secondhand smoke—that it can increase the risk for miscarriage, sudden infant death syndrome [SIDS], low birth weight and premature birth. Now, new research suggests that secondhand smoke might be every bit as damaging to a fetus as if the mother were inhaling the smoke directly from a cigarette.

Smoking or being exposed to second hand smoke while pregnant can lead to numerous problems with a baby, including SIDS, a low birth weight, premature death, and/or miscarriage.

- In March 2005, the *Washington Post* ran an article by Jennifer Huget about the effects of smoking cigarettes. Part of the article concerned how smoking affects pets:

If Sue Goodman were to quit smoking today, she said, it wouldn't be for herself; it would be for her husband and dog. Her last dog died of lung cancer, she explained. "I'm a heavy smoker. I know that's what killed him."

Goodman doesn't wish the same fate on her 4-year-old Chesapeake Bay retriever, Bo. But still she smokes—as she's been doing, at the rate of two

Secondhand smoke can affect pets negatively as well, causing lung cancer and death.

or more packs of More Menthol 120s a day, for 56 years (give or take a handful of periods when she tried to quit). That's about 817,600 cigarettes.

• On August 11, 1997, *The New Straits Times,* a Malaysian newspaper, ran this story about cigarette-induced death:

Fatal Smoking Contest, HONG KONG: A young man died and his friend suffered serious poisoning in a match in central China to see who could smoke more cigarettes, a report said yesterday. Liao Youchuan, 19, died after smoking 100 cigarettes in the match, while his friend, Zhang Chunyong, 21, suffered poisoning after smoking 80 cigarettes in Xiangyang county in Hubei province, the Chinese-language *Express Daily* said in a report. The young farmers started smoking one cigarette after another in "a competition out of boredom," but with encouragement from excited spectators, they went on to smoking several cigarettes at a time.

Both people and pets have suffered from cigarette use and paid the price with illness and death, but there are also other costs.

Personal Costs

A U.S. Navy study found that people who smoke experience lower job-performance ratings and

Annual Cost of Heart Diseases
• 685,089 deaths (49 percent men, 51 percent women)
• $142.5 billion (including health care services, medications, and lost productivity)

(Source: Centers for Disease Control and Prevention)

lower pay than people who never smoked. According to the report:

> Compared with never smokers, daily smokers at entry into the US Navy had subsequent career outcomes consistently indicating poorer job performance (e.g., early *attrition* prior to serving a full-term enlistment, more likely to have a less-than-honorable discharge, more demotions and desertions, lower achieved paygrade and less likely to re-enlist). Other types of smokers consistently fell between never and daily smokers on career outcome measures.

Some costs of smoking, such as the cost of buying cigarettes, are easy to measure in dollars. Other expenses, particularly the costs to a smoker's health, are more difficult to measure in monetary terms. Many of these smoking consequences have been recognized for years:

- In 1953, Dr. Irving S. Wright of Cornell University Medical College, reported cigarettes caused heart disease.
- According to the CDC, "Since 1964, 29 Surgeon General's reports on smoking and health have concluded that tobacco use is the single most avoidable cause of disease, disability, and death in the United States."
- By 1987, researchers knew that quitting smoking decreased the chance of getting heart disease, lung cancer, and other cancers.
- British researchers concluded in 2000, "Each cigarette smoked decreases the person's expected lifespan by 11 minutes."

On top of all the negative health effects that can result from smoking, there is also the huge economic cost. Smoking is an expensive habit to maintain.

- In 2007, the CDC reported, "Each year, an estimated 438,000 people in the United States die prematurely from smoking or exposure to secondhand smoke, and another 8.6 million have a serious illness caused by smoking."

A number of factors involving cigarettes increase the risk for disease. The primary culprit, however, is cigarette smoke.

Firsthand Smoke

Research shows that the initial drawing in of smoke through a cigarette has ill health effects. The CDC named lung cancer, other forms of lung disease, heart disease, and strokes as the primary causes of deaths attributed to cigarette smoking in the United States, and estimates the U.S. medical cost to treat illness caused by smoking at more than $75 billion per year. According to the

Smoking can cause heart disease, as well as other health problems like lung disease and stroke.

CDC, "The total economic costs associated with cigarette smoking are estimated at $7.18 per pack of cigarettes sold in the United States."

Today, the companies that manufacture cigarettes recognize the dangers of smoking. In 2007, Philip Morris USA, one of the largest cigarette makers posted to its company Web site:

> Philip Morris USA (PM USA) agrees with the overwhelming medical and scientific consensus that cigarette smoking causes lung cancer, heart disease, emphysema and other serious diseases in smokers. Smokers are far more likely to develop such serious diseases than non-smokers.

Lung Cancer and Lung Disease

For the five-year period from 1997 to 2001, the CDC reported that the leading cause of disease among smokers was lung disease, and the leading cause of death among smokers was lung cancer.

Heart Attacks and Strokes

"Heart disease is the leading cause of death for both women and men in the United States," reported the CDC in 2007. According to the American Heart Association (AHA), diseases of the heart, also known as cardiovascular disease, include high blood pressure, heart attack, reduced blood flow to the heart, and stroke. The AHA defines heart attacks as "death of or damage to part of the heart muscle due to an insufficient blood supply." Findings posted to the AHA

Web site in 2007 say, "Heart attacks occur when one of the coronary arteries that supply blood to the heart muscle is blocked. Blockage is usually caused from a buildup of plaque (deposits of fat-like substances)." Cigarette smoking is a major cause of coronary artery disease, which leads to heart attack. "Smoking increases blood pressure, decreases exercise tolerance and increases the tendency for blood to clot. Smoking also increases the risk of recurrent coronary heart disease after *bypass surgery*."

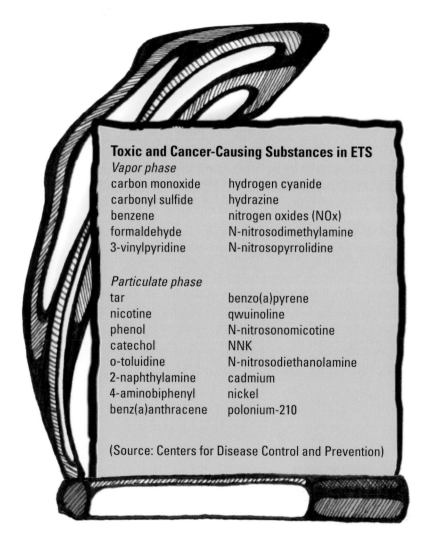

Toxic and Cancer-Causing Substances in ETS
Vapor phase

carbon monoxide	hydrogen cyanide
carbonyl sulfide	hydrazine
benzene	nitrogen oxides (NOx)
formaldehyde	N-nitrosodimethylamine
3-vinylpyridine	N-nitrosopyrrolidine

Particulate phase

tar	benzo(a)pyrene
nicotine	qwuinoline
phenol	N-nitrosonomicotine
catechol	NNK
o-toluidine	N-nitrosodiethanolamine
2-naphthylamine	cadmium
4-aminobiphenyl	nickel
benz(a)anthracene	polonium-210

(Source: Centers for Disease Control and Prevention)

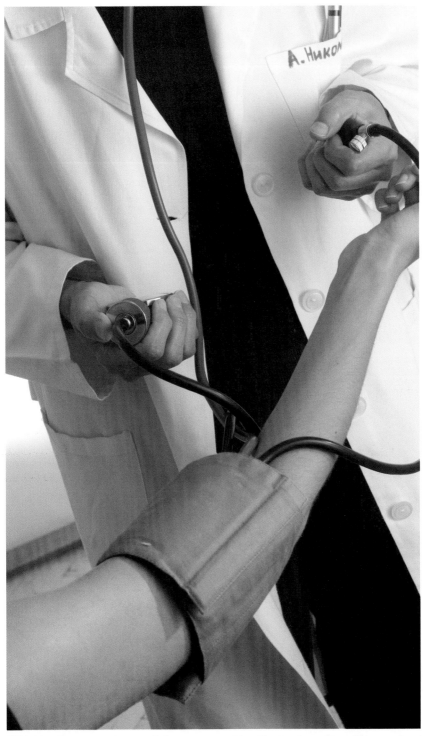

High blood pressure is one of the common side effects of smoking. This can lead to other, more serious health problems, like cardiac arrest.

The AHA defines strokes as "an interruption of blood flow to the brain causing paralysis, slurred speech and/or altered brain function." Cigarette smoking increases the risk of stroke. "The nicotine and carbon monoxide in cigarette smoke damage the cardiovascular system in many ways," explains the AHA. This risk is increased in women who smoke and use oral contraceptives.

Other Diseases and Effects

Smoking cigarettes has also been found to cause mouth disease and changes to skin, hair, and nails. The American Dental Association (ADA) says smoking causes

Smoking results in a decrease in the blood flowing throughout the skin, which can lead to wrinkles. The skin and nails also become discolored and yellow.

periodontal diseases, damages gum tissue by affecting the attachment of bone and soft tissue to teeth, hinders the ability to taste and smell, and leads to oral cancer.

Mayo Clinic dermatologist Lawrence Gibson says smoking causes wrinkles by impairing blood flow to the skin, depleting skin of oxygen and nutrients, and damaging collagen and elastin, the fibers that give skin its strength and elasticity. "As a result, skin begins to sag and wrinkle prematurely," the dermatologist says. Gibson also explains that facial expressions made while smoking, "such as pursing your lips when inhaling and squinting your eyes to keep out smoke," may promote the formation of wrinkles.

Apparently there isn't much a smoker can do to prevent his fingernails from becoming yellow. "As for the impact of nonyellowing top coats or enamel formulas, most experts agree that these may work to counteract the effects of environmental factors (such as the sun), but generally don't prevent yellowing of the nails caused by smoking," concluded reporter Tracy Molin in a 2007 article in *Nailpro*, a nail salon journal.

Cigarette smoking affects more people than just smokers. Smoke from cigarettes causes disease, death, and high financial costs to others in society as well.

Societal Costs

Cigarette smoking affects family members who must care for smoking relatives who become ill. Coworkers shoulder extra responsibilities and employers spend more money to hire workers to fill in for those who

Asthma is one of the common consequences of smoking. This can result from being exposed to secondhand smoke as well as inhaling the smoke from a cigarette directly.

miss work because of smoking-related illnesses. Insurance costs increase for everyone. However, some people think the greatest problem for society may be the same as the greatest problem for smokers: cigarette smoke.

Secondhand Smoke

When nonsmokers breathe in cigarette smoke, they, too, can develop diseases. These diseases range from asthma to lung damage to lung cancer. In his comprehensive work *The Cigarette Century*, tobacco historian Allan M. Brandt notes that environmental tobacco smoke (ETS), commonly known as secondhand smoke, contains 86 percent carbon monoxide. In 1992, the Environmental Protection Agency (EPA) labeled tobacco smoke a Class A human-lung *carcinogen*. Class A carcinogens are those substances that have achieved the greatest scientific certainty of cancer causation, according to the EPA. The EPA studied ETS in 1993 and concluded that "approximately 3,000 American nonsmokers die each year from lung cancer caused by secondhand smoke." The study found that children exposed to ETS suffer from increased rates of asthma, bronchitis, pneumonia, and sudden infant death syndrome, thus confirming what other groups had determined a decade earlier.

"More than 126 million nonsmoking Americans, including children and adults, are regularly exposed to secondhand smoke," concluded the

Annual Cost of Smoking to Nonsmokers
- 3,000 deaths due to lung cancer
- 35,000 deaths due to heart disease
- 150,000 to 300,000 lower-respiratory tract infections in children

(Source: Centers for Disease Control and Prevention, 2008)

CDC in 2007. This exposure leads to infections, cancer, and a cost of $92 billion per year due to lost productivity for illness and treatment.

For many years the tobacco industry disputed findings linking ETS to disease. The major cigarette companies Philip Morris, R. J. Reynolds, and Lorillard established the Center for Indoor Air Research (CIAR). CIAR studies concluded, "There are many other things to blame for poor indoor air quality, and tobacco smoke is only a small part of the problem."

Cigarette manufacturers are now admitting the adverse effects of ETS on public health. Philip Morris USA included this statement on its corporate Web site in 2007: "We also believe that where smoking is permitted, the government should require the posting of warning notices that communicate public health officials' conclusions that secondhand smoke causes disease in non-smokers."

In 2007, *Tobacco Control*, a journal for health professionals, published research on residual tobacco smoke (RTS), the smoke that remains in a smoker's lungs after finishing a cigarette. According to that research, even RTS contributes to indoor air pollution:

These data reveal a definite although marginal, role of RTS as a source of hidden indoor pollution. Further studies are needed to understand the relevance of this contribution in smoke-free premises in terms of risk exposure; however, waiting for about 2 min before re-entry after the last puff would be enough to avoid an unwanted additional exposure for non-smokers.

Children of Smokers

Though ETS affects all people, children of smokers are at greatest risk because of their long-term exposure to smoking. The first major report on smoking's effect on the children of smokers, released in 1986 by the National Academy of Sciences, showed that children of smokers are twice as likely to suffer respiratory illness as are children of nonsmokers.

Women who smoke while they are pregnant pass on smoke and chemicals to the unborn child. According to the AHA in 2007, "Women who smoke during pregnancy can cause permanent *vascular* damage in their children—increasing their risk for stroke and heart attack."

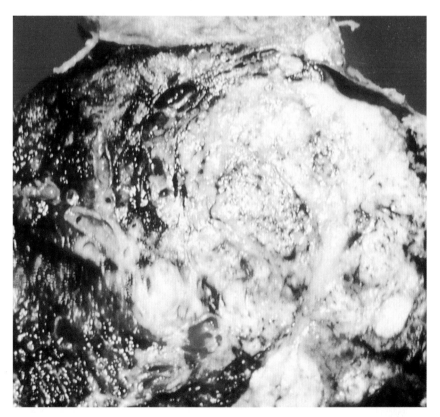

The cross section of a smoker's lung. Smoke remains in a smoker's lungs even after they are finished smoking, causing the build up of tars and other contaminants that appear as black spots in this photograph.

In other words, the effects of smoking during pregnancy carry over to the infant. A 2006 CDC study found that smoking by women during pregnancy can cause Sudden Infant Death Syndrome (SIDS), and that infants exposed to secondhand smoke after birth are also at a greater risk for SIDS. Furthermore, infants who died from SIDS had higher levels of nicotine in their lungs than those who died of other causes.

Children of smokers are at a huge risk of developing problems because of secondhand smoke, due to their constant exposure to the harmful chemicals.

By 2007, the EPA had published more than seven thousand documents on the effects of tobacco on indoor air pollution. Clearly, the most effective way to reduce the risk for smoking-related illnesses, both for smokers and for others, is to quit smoking. But even that can be expensive.

Effects of ETS on Children
Children exposed to ETS experience an increase in:

• asthma
• bronchitis and pneumonia
• middle-ear Infections
• sudden infant death syndrome

(Source: Environmental Protection Agency, 2008)

CHAPTER

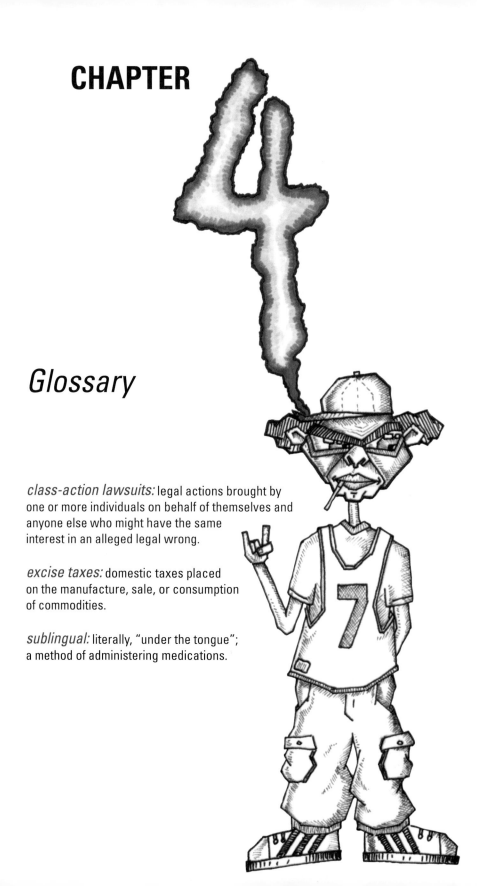

Glossary

class-action lawsuits: legal actions brought by one or more individuals on behalf of themselves and anyone else who might have the same interest in an alleged legal wrong.

excise taxes: domestic taxes placed on the manufacture, sale, or consumption of commodities.

sublingual: literally, "under the tongue"; a method of administering medications.

The Cost of Quitting and Prevention

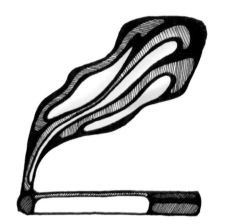

When it comes to quitting smoking, the physical benefits are far greater than any financial expense. Each year thousands of people take the first steps toward ending this costly habit.

USA Today reporter W. Reed Moran wrote in 2002 about the challenge for one actress to quit smoking:

> "I smoked for 23 years, three packs a day," says [*Law & Order* actress S. Epatha] Merkerson. "Then one day I woke up and simply couldn't breathe. I felt as if an elephant was sitting on my chest."
>
> Merkerson got the wake up call she needed, and quit smoking that day. That was eight years ago, but she still remembers that quitting wasn't easy.

"I'd tried to quit several times before," says Merkerson. "I tried every trick and smoking cessation program from the ridiculous to the sublime."

Initially, even the knowledge that her sister was suffering from smoking-induced lung cancer wasn't sufficient to make Merkerson drop the habit.

"It's hard to believe in retrospect, but my sister had been diagnosed with lung cancer for three years before I was able to quit," says Merkerson. "That gives you some idea how insidiously addictive nicotine can be."

Ron Monroe lit his first cigarette at age twelve. "My dad and mom both smoked. It seemed like everybody smoked back then," he recalled. Forty years later, Ron was smoking at least three packs of cigarettes a day. "I smoked in the morning with my coffee, after every meal, and to relax," he said. "Anywhere I was permitted to smoke, I smoked. That was a lot of cigarettes in a ten-hour day."

Then he considered the cost of smoking: "I was retired, lived on a lake, and wanted a new boat. My wife and I were both smokers, and our health started to bother us. We added up how much we spent a month on cigarettes, almost four hundred dollars, and it was enough to pay for a brand new boat plus the insurance, with plenty left over." Ron said, "Between coughing and the cost of cigarettes, we decided to quit smoking." Then they bought their boat.

In his 1988 book *Merchants of Death*, Larry C. White included the story of Olympic diver Greg Louganis, who began smoking when he was just eight years old. Louganis kept his habit a secret from his diving coach. One day after diving practice, the world-famous athlete

Many people start smoking at extremely young ages, before they become fully aware of all the negative consequences the habit will have on them and the people around them.

Trying to quit smoking can lead to depression as the body starts going through nicotine withdrawal.

saw a twelve-year-old boy smoking. "When I asked him why, he said he wanted to be just like me!" said Louganis. He added, "I realized that in a way *I* was a 'Marlboro Man' of sorts."

That incident caused Louganis to quit smoking and to volunteer for the American Cancer Society (ACS).

People have many reasons for quitting smoking. Those who quit can pay quite a price in terms of time and money to do so, but that expense is minor compared to how much they save by not buying cigarettes and how many years each former smoker adds to her life.

Personal Costs

According to a 2006 report in the *Journal of the American Medical Association*, most adult smokers report that they want to quit smoking, and "most ex-smokers try several times, often as many as eight to ten times, before they are able to quit for good." Another organization came to the same conclusion. The Smoking Cessation Leadership Center found that less than 5 percent of smokers are able to quit without assistance. Why is quitting cigarette use so difficult?

A Brown & Williamson (B&W) internal

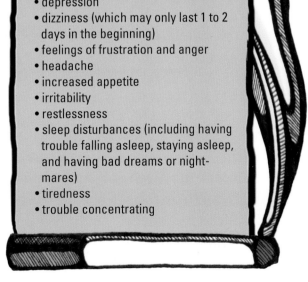

Nicotine Withdrawal Symptoms
- depression
- dizziness (which may only last 1 to 2 days in the beginning)
- feelings of frustration and anger
- headache
- increased appetite
- irritability
- restlessness
- sleep disturbances (including having trouble falling asleep, staying asleep, and having bad dreams or nightmares)
- tiredness
- trouble concentrating

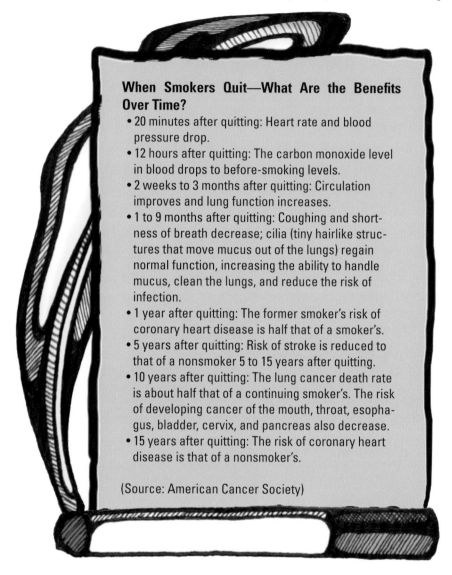

When Smokers Quit—What Are the Benefits Over Time?
- 20 minutes after quitting: Heart rate and blood pressure drop.
- 12 hours after quitting: The carbon monoxide level in blood drops to before-smoking levels.
- 2 weeks to 3 months after quitting: Circulation improves and lung function increases.
- 1 to 9 months after quitting: Coughing and shortness of breath decrease; cilia (tiny hairlike structures that move mucus out of the lungs) regain normal function, increasing the ability to handle mucus, clean the lungs, and reduce the risk of infection.
- 1 year after quitting: The former smoker's risk of coronary heart disease is half that of a smoker's.
- 5 years after quitting: Risk of stroke is reduced to that of a nonsmoker 5 to 15 years after quitting.
- 10 years after quitting: The lung cancer death rate is about half that of a continuing smoker's. The risk of developing cancer of the mouth, throat, esophagus, bladder, cervix, and pancreas also decrease.
- 15 years after quitting: The risk of coronary heart disease is that of a nonsmoker's.

(Source: American Cancer Society)

memo dated July 17, 1963, provided one answer: "Nicotine is addictive." The writer continued, "We are, then, in the business of selling nicotine, an addictive drug effective in the release of stress mechanisms." Nine years later, in a speech at the Philip Morris Research Center, William L. Dunn Jr. reasserted the nicotine effect: "No one has ever become a cigarette smoker by smoking cig-arettes without nicotine."

But despite the addictive quality and physical effects of nicotine use, more and more people quit smoking every year.

Deciding to Quit

Some smokers look at the many costs of smoking and decide to quit. They consider the cost to their health, their wallet, or their reputation, and make up their minds to stop smoking. The CDC's National Health Interview Surveys found that in 1965, 42 percent of Americans smoked cigarettes; in 1985, that figure dropped to 30 per-cent; and by 2004, just 20 percent of Americans smoked cigarettes. During that same period, the number of for-mer smokers grew from 13 percent to 21 percent.

For many smokers, ending cigarette use is a difficult decision. Their bodies, accustomed to the chemicals and effects of smoking cigarettes, experience withdrawal symptoms such as depression, headaches, and increased appe-tite, all of which must be overcome in order to break the nicotine habit.

To help in their efforts to quit smoking, many former smokers alter their daily routines. For exam-ple, some purposely stay away from situations they usually associated with having a cigarette. Most smokers who want to stop need to bring in outside help, ranging in cost from

Four Keys to Quitting

1. Making the decision to quit
2. Setting a quit date and choos-ing a quit plan
3. Dealing with withdrawal
4. Staying quit (maintenance)

(Source: American Cancer Society)

free advice to hundreds of dollars for medical prescriptions.

For all former smokers, the time and money spent to stop smoking brings long-term benefits, including lower heart rate, lower blood pressure, and cleaner lungs. According to the ACS, within fifteen years of quitting smoking, the risk of heart attacks to former smokers equals that of nonsmokers.

Pressure to Quit

In 1988, U.S. Surgeon General C. Everett Koop wrote the foreword to *Merchants of Death: The American Tobacco Industry.* He discussed his role in the campaign to educate Americans about the effects of tobacco use: "In addi-

Many homes have smoke-free rules that prevent people from smoking in the house. This pressure to stop smoking can help many people find the motivation to quit.

tion to my own annual reports on smoking and health, I announced the goal of making the United States a smoke-free society by the year 2000."

By 2007, most homes in the United States had "no smoking" rules. According to CDC data, "Nearly three out of four U.S. households do not allow smoking anywhere and any time in the home." The CDC found that the proportion of homes with smoke-free rules increased in every state from 1992 to 2003. Kentucky—a major tobacco-growing state—reported the lowest proportion of homes with smoke-free home rules, yet the number of smoke-free homes in the "Bluegrass State" increased from 26 percent to 53 percent during the eleven-year study. Utah reported the highest proportion of smoke-free home rules at 89 percent.

A nationwide no-smoking event started when a Minnesota newspaper editor named Lynn R. Smith called for a Don't Smoke Day in 1974. The California division of the ACS followed with a no-smoking day on November 18, 1976, which led to the now annual nationwide ACS Great American Smokeout, first held in 1977.

For one day a year, the World Health Organization (WHO) also holds a global no-smoking day. Since 1987, countries around the globe have celebrated WHO's World No Tobacco Day on May 31.

The Campaign for Tobacco-Free Kids launched an annual tobacco-awareness campaign in 1995 called Kick Butts Day (KBD). Each March, young people across the United States send a powerful message to elected officials at all levels to step up the fight to reduce tobacco use. KBD activities have included flag displays to represent annual deaths from tobacco and secondhand smoke, mock funerals for the Marlboro Man, and screenings of student-created tobacco-prevention commercials.

Support Groups

Many people attempt to quit smoking on their own. Despite good intentions, going it alone is not an effective way to stop smoking. According to a 2000 article in the journal *Thorax*, only 3 percent of those trying to quit succeed using willpower alone. A doctor's help can increase the success rate to 5 percent. With support from a specialist, 10 percent become former smokers. The ACS recommends the support of family and friends as a tool to quit smoking: "Many former smokers say a support

Family support can be extremely important in quitting smoking.

network of family and friends was very important during their quit attempt."

To provide the support to quit, a free nationwide telephone counseling system took effect in 2004. States receive funds as part of the CDC's National Tobacco Control Program to link callers to free counseling. People who call the national quitline, 1-800-QUITNOW, receive assistance and information about local smoking-cessation resources.

Not all support groups are free. According to a 2006 article by the *Pittsburgh Post-Gazette*, for example, an inpatient program offered by the Mayo Clinic cost $4,500. Because quitting smoking usually results in long-term health benefits, the cost of some smoking-cessation programs may be covered by health insurance plans.

Nicotine Replacement Therapy

For some people, small amounts of nicotine introduced into the body can relieve the craving to smoke and increase the likelihood of smoking-cessation success. According to researcher Andrew Molyneux, the use of nicotine replacement therapy (NRT) can increase the success rate to 18 percent when compared to using verbal support alone.

NRT is safer than obtaining nicotine through smoking because consumers are not exposed to the thousands of other dangerous chemicals that are present in tobacco products. Forms of NRT include gums, patches, sprays, inhalers, *sublingual* tablets, and lozenges. Most are readily available to adults without a prescription, but young people need to have a prescription in order to obtain NRTs.

Non-Nicotine Medications

For some people, support groups and NRT are not enough to quit for good. In these cases, doctors sometimes prescribe a non-nicotine medication that blocks the desire to smoke. Bupropion, clonidine, and nortriptyline are among the medications used in the United States that have been proven effective for smoking cessation.

Societal Costs

It's a fact of life: Children who grow up with parents who smoke are more likely to become smokers themselves. In turn, children who smoke may pass the habit on to their peers, and this impacts society as a whole. In May 2007, the Institute of Medicine released a study titled *Ending the Tobacco Problem: A Blueprint for the Nation.* The researchers concluded:

> Studies indicate that 12-year-old children of parents who smoke are roughly twice as likely to begin smoking between the ages of 13 and 21 years as those whose parents do not smoke.
>
> Adolescents aged 15 to 17 years were 74 percent less likely to be smokers if they lived in houses with smoking restrictions.

Adults who smoke, those who quit, and those who never smoked all influence the next generation.

Never Starting

The number of people who have chosen never to smoke has increased every year. Statistics from the CDC show that in 1965, 44 percent of Americans had never smoked. By 2005, that number had grown to 60 percent. Among people between the ages of eighteen and twenty-four, the CDC statistics show that, in 1965, 48 percent of young Americans had never smoked. By 2005, that number had grown to 70 percent. So the good news is, most young people are choosing to avoid cigarettes.

Society can avoid many future costs of smoking by encouraging individuals not to smoke. In 1997, cigarette companies agreed to pay billions of dollars toward smoking prevention programs when they signed the Master Settlement Agreement (MSA) with forty-six states and some U.S. territories (agreements had previously been reached with four states).

The Master Settlement Agreement and Individual Lawsuits
When cigarette manufacturers and states agreed to the Master Settlement Agreement, it didn't mean that all legal action against the companies was over. Individuals were still allowed to file suit. Though large individual awards have made the news, most individuals lose their cases against the cigarette manufacturers. Even when large awards are made, most cases have been overturned on appeal or the monetary damages awarded by sympathetic juries have been dramatically reduced.

The Marlboro Man

In 1992, the *New York Times* ran an article about a famous advertising campaign by cigarette maker Philip Morris. The ad featured a rugged, smoking cowboy known as the Marlboro Man. Over the years of the ad campaign, several models played the role. Here's what this article said happened to one of them:

The Marlboro man image has proven so powerful and seductive that Marlboro's parent company, Philip Morris, guards it zealously. The models, most of whom are actual cowboys, "are sworn to secrecy" about all aspects of their work, a company spokesman said. But just before he died of lung cancer last

The Marlboro Man made smoking romantic. However, the reality is that many of
the Marlboro Men have died of lung problems.

July at 51 years old, Wayne McLaren went very public, saying he had worked briefly as a cowboy-model for Marlboro. At the end of a life spent around the edge of celebrity, Mr. McLaren's anti-smoking advocacy made him a romantic hero of another sort. "I'm dying proof," he told interviewers before his death, "that smoking will kill you."

In September 1996, the *Houston Chronicle* ran a story with the headline "Marlboro Man duped, widow says/ Suit seeks damages from tobacco firms." The article read in part:

The stoical Marlboro Man, tall and alone in the saddle, image of all that is masculine and strong, was actually an actor choking his way through pack after pack of cigarettes while fussy movie directors tried to get the smoke to rise just so and the ash to tip in just the right direction, according to a wrongful death suit.

It did him in, according to Lilo McLean, his widow, who is suing Philip Morris Cos. Inc. and other tobacco companies in a lawsuit filed in federal court in Marshall.

"They used him as a pawn to make everybody smoke," said Jack Baldwin, a Marshall attorney representing Mrs. McLean. "They didn't even tell him the danger. He was duped as well."

Actor David McLean, who portrayed the Marlboro Man in television commercials beginning in the early 1960s, died of lung cancer last year at age 73. His widow's lawsuit seeks unspecified money damages, claiming Philip Morris should have warned McLean, who started smoking at age 12, that the cigarettes he was smoking might kill him.

The lawsuit by one Marlboro Man's wife marked the end of an era of lawsuits against cigarette companies that had started more than a decade earlier. Lawsuits against cigarette companies eventually led to the MSA. Today, the money from that agreement continues to fund educational programs to persuade people to quit smoking or never to start.

The Master Settlement Agreement

Lawsuits against cigarette manufacturers focused on two main issues: marketing techniques and knowledge of nicotine's addictive effects. In the 1980s, cigarette companies won lawsuits that could have cost them millions of dollars. On June 20, 1997, faced with the probability of *class-action lawsuits* from many states, cigarette companies agreed to an out-of-court settlement. According to the agreement, they would pay $365.5 billion over the next twenty-five years to compensate states for smoking-cessation programs and health care costs.

Why did tobacco companies fear they would begin to lose lawsuits and agree to make a deal? One key turning point occurred

So Where's the Money Going?

Studies have shown that states have spent only a small proportion of the money awarded as part of the Master Settlement Agreement on smoking-cessation programs. Each state can determine how to spend the money it receives. Among the items and programs that have been funded by settlement money are:

- school buildings
- harbor renovations
- Medicaid dental services
- psychiatric care for prison inmates
- golf carts and golf course irrigation
- broadband cable networks

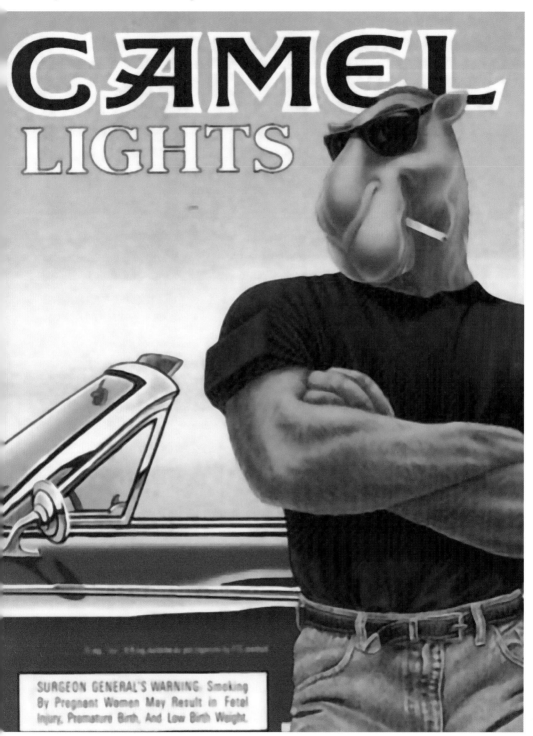

Joe Camel was another attempt by tobacco companies to make smoking look appealing, in this case especially to younger audiences.

in 1994, when an anonymous package arrived at the University of California at San Francisco (UCSF). The contents shed light on the tobacco industry's knowledge of nicotine.

Legacy Tobacco Documents Library

Professor Stanton Glantz, who now directs the Tobacco Research and Education Center, received 4,000 pages of secret tobacco industry documents at his UCSF office in May 1994, from a then-anonymous source named "Mr. Butts," after a character from Gary Trudeau's "Doonesbury" comic strip. These "Cigarette Papers" sparked major headlines across the nation and later became the focus of a major motion picture.

The UCSF founded the Legacy Tobacco Documents Library with those papers and released the documents to the public via the Internet. By May 2003, the library holdings exceeded 36 million pages of tobacco-industry documents related to advertising, manufacturing, marketing, sales, and scientific research concerning tobacco products.

Public accessibility of industry documents allowed the world to see memos, ads, and research about the effects of nicotine. With such clear evidence of industry knowledge, tobacco companies became more vulnerable to lawsuits, and the MSA was negotiated to reduce the chances of large jury awards.

Prevention Efforts

Smoking-prevention efforts, financed by the MSA and cigarette taxes, are aimed at smokers and young people. According to the CDC, these programs cost a fraction of the money available to fund them. CDC statistics show that combined state tobacco-prevention program funding peaked at about $750 million in 2002 and fell to $538 million in 2005. The CDC reported, "States are currently spending only 2.8% of the $21.7 billion available through tobacco *excise taxes* and settlement funds on tobacco prevention and control."

The national quitline effort, free to callers, costs an estimated $3.2 billion per year to operate, according to a 2002 report by the Group Health Center for Health Promotion. Finally, according to researchers for *ABC of Smoking Cessation*, the average cost for smoking-cessation programs is $3,779 for each person who stops smoking.

The cost of quitting and prevention fit hand in hand. The money spent by each smoker who quits smoking is relatively low compared to the societal expense of prevention. Much of the money used to pay for such programs comes from tobacco companies through the MSA. Of course, tobacco companies obtain that money by selling cigarettes to consumers. So ultimately, the cost of prevention programs falls mostly on tobacco users.

CHARTER

Glossary

deforestation: the process of clearing forests.

hectares: a metric unit of measurement equal to 2.471 acres or 10,000 square miles.

The Cost of Purchase and Production

The smoking habit generates many costs, both to individuals and to our environment. The cost to purchase cigarettes adds up over time, according to a 2005 *Washington Post* article, which read in part:

Warning: Cigarette smoking may be hazardous to your wealth.

At least that's the claim of Jay Zagorsky, an economist at Ohio State University's Center for Human Resource Research.

Zagorsky found that the net worth of nonsmokers is roughly 50 percent higher than that of light smokers and about double the wealth of heavy puffers. He also found

Smoking is an extremely expensive habit: smokers are likely to be less
economically well-off than their nonsmoking counterparts.

that the wealth gap grows by about $410 for each year that a person continues to smoke—changes that could not be explained away by differences in education levels, income or other factors associated with wealth accumulation.

Zagorsky said that federal statistics on cigarette spending revealed an interesting pattern: The wealth reductions were roughly equal to how much smokers spend on their habit, suggesting that smokers buy cigarettes with money they would otherwise save, rather than with cash they would have spent on entertainment or on other non-wealth-producing goods or services.

In other words, a small but significant portion of their wealth goes up in smoke each year.

Cigarettes generate tons of trash that either degrades the environment or is cleaned up by volunteers. According to the Ocean Conservancy Web site:

In 1986, a staff member of the Ocean Conservancy was appalled by the amount of trash she found littering the shores of South Padre Island, Texas. She took responsible action by organizing a beach cleanup. In three hours, 2,800 Texans picked up 124 tons [112,600 kg] of trash from 122 miles [196 km] of coastline. With that, Ocean Conservancy's International Coastal Cleanup (ICC) was born.

What started as a local beach cleanup in Texas grew to become the largest one-day volunteer effort in the world to benefit the earth's waterways. Each year, on a Saturday in mid-September, hundreds of thousands of volunteers around the world clean up debris in and

**Annual Revenue for the Top
Five Cigarette Manufacturers**

• Vector Group Ltd.: $52.4 million
• Altria Group Inc. (Philip Morris
  USA): $10.4 billion
• Lowes Corporation: $2.49 billion
• Houchens Industries: $2.36 bil-
  lion
• Reynolds American Inc.: $1.2
  billion

(Source: Centers for Disease Control and Prevention, 2007)

around waterways. To date, ICC has organized 6.2 million volunteers and collected 109 million pounds (49.5 million kg) of debris along 179,000 miles (288,000 km) of beaches and waterways in 127 nations.

In 2005, volunteers collected 8.2 million pounds (3.7 million kg) of debris. Cigarette trash comprised approximately 2.4 million pounds (1.1 million kg) of the total debris collected. According to the ICC, of the total debris collected, 29 percent was from smoking-related activities, including lighters, cigarette filters, and cigarette packaging.

Those numbers represent just the cigarette debris that is recovered and then properly discarded. No one can calculate how many discarded cigarette filters, packages, and lighters still litter the environment.

The U.S. Department of Agriculture (USDA) tracks crops grown and sold across the country. In 2006, tobacco ranked among the country's top-ten cash crops. In fact, enough tobacco was grown to make 484 billion cigarettes. Americans bought about three-fourths of those cigarettes, and people in other countries purchased the remaining one-fourth. According to the CDC, the total amount of money spent on cigarettes in 2005 was $82 billion!

Tobacco is one of the country's top ten cash crops, meaning that it is a major contributor to America's economy.

Personal Costs

According to the CDC's 2006 statistics, one in five American adults smokes cigarettes. These 45 million people purchase billions of cigarettes.

Consumer Costs

In 2006, the average cost of a pack of cigarettes was $4.26. According to surveys by the National Institute on Drug Abuse (NIDA), the average smoker purchases 265 packs of cigarettes and spends about $1,129 on them each year.

Personal-finance columnist Michelle Singletary met with Carl Chandler and his wife in 2007 to help them create a budget. She found that a significant part of their income went toward their smoking habit. Singletary's column ran in the *Washington Post* and read, in part:

About three fourths of the cigarettes produced in the United States are purchased by Americans.

Chandler spent about $1,000 last year on his smoking habit. What if he saved that money?

If Chandler, who is 38, stopped smoking and invested that $1,000 every year in a 401(k), with a rate of return of 8 percent, he would have more than $100,000 by age 65.

"You think this is just pocket money," Chandler said. "But it's a good savings that you can put aside."

When a consumer puts down his money for a pack of cigarettes, it's obvious that the retailer will make some money from the sale. The federal government, state government, and manufacturers also earn income from the sale.

The federal government receives a set tax on each cigarette pack. In 1997, Congress passed a law setting the tax at $0.39 per pack, and the amount has stayed the same ever since. This money goes into the federal government's general fund.

Each state government sets its own tax rate on cigarettes and tobacco products. In 2007, these taxes ranged from a low of $.07 for each pack of cigarettes in South Carolina (a tobacco-growing state) to a high of $2.58 in New Jersey. Many states spend a portion of this revenue on programs to educate people about the effects of smoking.

Cigarette manufacturers and retailers that sell cigarettes share the bulk of the remainder of the purchase price. Most of the money goes to the manufacturers. According to some estimates, only 8 percent of the cost of a pack of cigarettes goes to the tobacco farmer.

Societal Costs

Tobacco impacts the environment at three stages: growing tobacco, manufacturing cigarettes, and consuming cigarettes. The process has a negative environmental impact at every stage.

Growing Tobacco

"Tobacco is a major U.S. industry," concluded a 2000 USDA report. Regarding cigarette sales, the report said, "These consumer expenditures support thousands of businesses that manufacture, transport, market, and sell these products, as well as some 90,000 farms that grow tobacco leaf." According to USDA data from 2004, farmers grew tobacco in twenty-one states, but two-thirds of all tobacco comes from Kentucky and North Carolina.

Worldwide, tobacco farming imposes a great environmental cost: *deforestation*. "Just as litter is an offshoot of tobacco consumption, so deforestation is the result of tobacco production," said geographer Helmut Geist of the University of Louvain in Belgium. According to research by Geist, published in *Tobacco Control*, "between 1991 and 1995 an estimated 200,000 *hectares* of forests worldwide were removed to make way for tobacco farming each year, mostly in developing countries in Africa, Asia, and Latin America."

The Cost to Cigarette Manufacturers

According to the USDA, Americans purchased 371 billion cigarettes in 2006. That year, just five companies produced 90 percent of all cigarettes made in the United States. The main costs to these companies involved marketing their tobacco products.

The tobacco industry employs approximately 32,680 people, according to the most recent numbers from the United States Department of Labor's Bureau of Labor

Statistics (BLS). More than half of these jobs involve the actual production of cigarettes. According to BLS data, cigarette manufacturers spend at least $1.2 billion to pay workers who make cigarettes.

Tobacco companies spend many times that amount to market cigarettes. According to the Federal Trade Commission (FTC) cigarette report for 2004–2005, the cigarette industry spent $13.11 billion on advertising. None of this money was spent to advertise cigarettes on radio or television because the Federal Cigarette Labeling Act banned such ads in 1971. Since then, the FTC has required health-warning labels on magazine, newspaper, and billboard advertising for cigarettes. In response, tobacco companies have spent less money on those types of ads. Today, the main ways tobacco companies promote their

The huge demand for tobacco has resulted in deforestation, as farmers destroy woodlands in order to develop more land for farming.

products are through price discounts, coupons, and free bonus cigarettes.

The Costs to the Environment

The environment pays a price for the manufacturing of cigarettes. The main cost to the environment is environmental waste. A spring 1999 study, published in *Tobacco Control* said the tobacco manufacturing process produced more than six thousand pounds (2,724 kg) of liquid, solid, and airborne waste. "Among those wastes, some materials, including nicotine, are designated by the EPA as Toxics Release Inventory (TRI) chemicals," said the researchers. These hazardous chemicals require special disposal.

The *Tobacco Control* researchers say waste also poses a risk for developing countries: "The tobacco industry is moving manufacturing processes to developing countries, and this has environmental consequences." These consequences are especially serious because developing nations may not have the money necessary to monitor the industry or to clean up the waste.

Besides the impact caused by producing cigarettes, consuming tobacco products also affects the environment. In 2007, the EPA reported:

> Smokers who flick cigarette filters out of a car window, stamp cigarettes out on a sidewalk, or dump out their car ashtrays in a parking lot contribute to the marine debris problem. Cigarette filters can wash or blow down storm drains that lead into our local waterways and eventually, the ocean.

Volunteers, such as those affiliated with the Ocean Conservancy's International Coastal Cleanup, have removed tons of litter from the beaches and shorelines of the United States.

Cigarettes are a huge cause of pollution. Butts easily find their way into waterways and oceans, where they can eventually wash up on beaches like this one.

Cost of Smoking

As discussed throughout this book, smoking places an enormous cost on individuals and society. Here we take one last look at the approximate annual costs:

- The cost of accidental smoking-material fires exceeds $400 million, more than one thousand injuries, and more than seven hundred deaths.
- The cost of cigarette-induced illnesses exceeds $167 billion, 1 million deaths, and 300,000 new illnesses.
- The cost of quitting averages nearly $4,000 per quitter, and smoking-prevention programs cost billions more. Most people consider the funds spent for quitting and prevention as money well spent, since it saves health care costs and human lives.
- The smoking costs associated with purchase and production include $82 billion spent to buy cigarettes, three tons (2,722 kg) of manufacturing waste, and more than eight tons (7,258 kg) of litter.

So the grand total is hundreds of billions of dollars in costs for use of 500 billion cigarettes. In a way, each cigarette smoked is like setting one dollar bill on fire. You could say that smoking burns an awful lot of money.

Further Reading

Anderson, Judith. *Smoking (It's Your Health)*. North Mankato, Minn.: Smart Apple Media, 2005.

Balkin, Karen, and Helen Cothran (eds.). *Tobacco and Smoking*. San Diego: Greenhaven Press, 2004.

Brandt, Allan M. *The Cigarette Century: The Rise, Fall, and Deadly Persistence of the Product that Defined America*. New York: Basic Books, 2007.

Haughten, Emma. *The Right to Smoke?* North Mankato, Minn.: Sea to Sea Publications, 2005.

Hurley, Jennifer A. (ed.). *Addiction: Opposing Viewpoints*. San Diego: Greenhaven Press, 2000.

Hyde, Margret O., and John F. Setaro. *Smoking 101: An Overview for Teens*. Minneapolis: Twenty-First Century Books, 2006.

Lobster Press (ed.). *Let's Clear the Air: 10 Reasons Not to Start Smoking*. Montreal, Quebec: Lobster Press, 2007.

Sanders, Pete, and Steve Myers. *Smoking (Choices and Decisions)*. North Mankato, Minn.: Stargazer Books, 2006.

Wagner, Susan. *Cigarette Country: Tobacco in American History and Politics*. New York: Praeger Publishers, 1971.

White, Larry C. *Merchants of Death: The American Tobacco Industry*. New York: Beech Tree Books, 1988.

For More Information

1–800–QUITNOW
www.smokefree.gov

American Cancer Society
www.cancer.org

American Heart Association
www.americanheart.org

American Lung Association
www.lungusa.org

Campaign for Tobacco-Free Kids
tobaccofreekids.org

Legacy Tobacco Documents Library
http://legacy.library.ucsf.edu

Smoke Free Homes Programs
www.epa.gov/smokefree

Smoke Free Kids
www.smokefreekids.com/kids.htm

Sparky the Fire Dog
www.sparky.org

Publisher's note:
The Web sites listed on this page were active at the time of publication. The publisher is not responsible for Web sites that have changed their addresses or discontinued operation since the date of publication. The publisher will review and update the Web-site list upon each reprint.

Bibliography

Adler, Margot. "Behind the Ever-Expanding American Dream House." *All Things Considered*, July 4, 2006. http://www.npr.org/templates/story/story. php?storyId=5525283.

American Cancer Society. "Guide to Quitting Smoking." http://www.cancer.org/docroot/PED/content/PED_10_13X_Guide_for_Quitting_Smoking. asp?sitearea=PED.

American Cancer Society, "Leading Sites of New Cancer Cases and Deaths—2007 Estimates." http://www.cancer.org/docroot/MED/content/downloads/MED_1_1x_CFF2007_Leading_Sites_New_Cases_Deaths_Estimates.asp.

American Cancer Society. "Smoking and Cancer Mortality Table," October 11, 2006. http://www.cancer.org/docroot/PED/content/PED_10_2X_Smoking_and_Cancer_Mortality_Table.asp.

American Dental Association. "Smoking (Tobacco) Cessation." http://www.ada.org/public/topics/smoking_tobacco_faq.asp.

American Heart Association. "Cigarette Smoking and Cardiovascular Diseases." http://www.americanheart. org/presenter.jhtml?identifier=4545.

American Heart Association. "Pregnant Smokers Raise Their Child's risk of Stroke, Heart Attack." http://www.americanheart.org/presenter. jhtml?identifier=3045781.

American Heart Association. "Stroke Risk Factors." http://www.americanheart.org/presenter. jhtml?identifier=4716.

Arakelian, Hourie. "Fire Chief Blames Fatal Apartment Fire on Cigarette." KCENTV.com, January 9, 2006. http://www.kcentv.com/news/local-article-arch. php?nid=8821.

Brender, Erin. "Smoking Cessation." *Journal of the American Medical Association* 296 (July 2006). http://jama.ama-assn.org/cgi/content/full/296/1/130.

Capehart, Thomas C. "Tobacco: Background." Environmental Research Service, U.S. Department of Agriculture, October 3, 2005. http://www.ers.usda. gov/Briefing/Tobacco/Background.htm.

Centers for Disease Control and Prevention. "Annual Deaths Attributable to Cigarette Smoking—United States, 1997–2001." http://www.cdc.gov/tobacco/ data_statistics/tables/health/attrdths.htm.

Centers for Disease Control and Prevention. "Fact Sheet: Adult Cigarette Smoking in the United States: Current Estimates." *Smoking and Tobacco*, November 2006. http://www.cdc.gov/tobacco/data_statistics/ Factsheets/adult_cig_smoking.htm.

Centers for Disease Control and Prevention. "Fact Sheet: Economic Facts About U.S. Tobacco Use and Tobacco Production." *Smoking & Tobacco Use*, July 2007. http://www.cdc.gov/tobacco/data_statistics/ Factsheets/economic_facts.htm.

Centers for Disease Control and Prevention. "Fact Sheet: Ventilation Does Not Effectively Protect Nonsmokers from Secondhand Smoke." *Smoking and Tobacco Use*, October 2006. http://www.cdc.gov/tobacco/data_statistics/Factsheets/Ventilation.htm.

Centers for Disease Control and Prevention. "More U.S. Households Adopting Smoke-Free Home Rules." http://www.cdc.gov/od/oc/media/pressrel/2007/r070524.htm.

Centers for Disease Control and Prevention. "Secondhand Smoke Causes Sudden Infant Death Syndrome." http://www.cdc.gov/tobacco/data_statistics/Factsheets/Sids.htm.

 "Cigarette Labeling and Advertising." US Code 15.36 (2005). http://uscode.house.gov/download/pls/15C36.txt.

Conway, Terry L., Susan I. Woodruff, and Linda K. Hervig. "Women's Smoking History Prior to Entering the US Navy: A Prospective Predictor of Performance." *Tobacco Control.* http://tobaccocontrol.bmj.com/cgi/content/abstract/16/2/79.

Environmental Protection Agency. "Enviro-Q: What Is the Number One Trash Item Found on Beaches?" May 18, 2007. http://www.epa.gov/epahome/eqanswer.html.

Federal Trade Commission. *Cigarette Report for 2004 and 2005.* http://www.ftc.gov/reports/tobacco/2007cigarette2004-2005.pdf.

Foreman, Linda F. "Tobacco Production Costs and Returns 2004." *Electronic Outlook Report from the Economic Research Service*, August 2006. http://www.ers.usda.gov/publications/tbs/aug06/tbs26001/tbs26001.pdf.

Gale, H. Frederick, Jr., Linda Foreman, and Thomas C. Capehart. "Tobacco and the Economy: Farms, Jobs, and Communities." ERS, USDA, 2000. http://www.ers.usda.gov/Publications/AER789.

Geist, Helmut J. "Global Assessment of Deforestation Related to Tobacco Farming." *Tobacco Control.* http://tobaccocontrol.bmj.com/cgi/content/abstract/8/1/18.

Gibson, Lawrence. "Smoking: How Does It Affect Your Skin?" Mayo Clinic. http://www.mayoclinic.com/health/smoking/AN00644.

Grant, Kelli B., "Get Rich, Quit Smoking." SmartMoney.com, Jan. 5, 2007. http://www.smartmoney.com/dealoftheday/index.cfm?story=20070105&pgnum=1.

Hall, John R. Hall, Jr. "The Total Cost of Fire in the United States." National Fire Protection Association, December 2006. http://www.nfpa.org/assets/files//PDF/totalcostsum.pdf.

Huget, Jennifer. "Smoke Gets in Their Eyes: Despite Overwhelming Evidence That Smoking Kills, 46 Million Still Do It. What Are They Thinking?" *Washington Post*, March 29, 2005. http://www.washingtonpost.com/ac2/wp-dyn/A8063-2005Mar28?language=printer.

Molyneux, Andrew. "ABC of Smoking Cessation: Nicotine Replacement Therapy." *BMJ* 328 (February 21, 2004). http://www.bmj.com/cgi/reprint/328/7437/454.pdf.

Moran, W. Reed. "S. Epatha Merkerson Campaigns Against Smoking." *USA Today*, April 4, 2002. http://www.usatoday.com/news/health/spotlight/2002/04/03-merkerson.htm.

National Association of Realtors. "Cigarette Smokers Have Tough Time Selling." *Daily Real Estate News*, National Association of Realtors, June 30, 2006. http://www.realtor.org/rmodaily.nsf/0/a4885f9204d949748625719d004d619e?OpenDocument.

National Fire Protection Association. "Selected Published Smoking-Material Fire Incidents." http://www.nfpa.org/assets/files//PDF/Smokingmaterialincidents.pdf.

National Institute on Drug Abuse. "NIDA InfoFacts: Cigarettes and Other Tobacco Products." http://www.nida.nih.gov/Infofacts/Tobacco.html.

Ocean Conservancy. "About the International Coastal Cleanup." http://www.oceanconservancy.org/site/News2?page=NewsArticle&id=8761.

Schutze, Jim. "Marlboro Man Duped, Widow Says/Suit Seeks Damages From Tobacco Firms." *Houston Chronicle*, Sept. 14, 1996. http://www.howarth-smith.com/News/news-49.htm.

"Secondhand Smoke." PhilipMorrisUSA.com, June 19, 2007. http://www.philipmorrisusa.com/en/health_issues/secondhand_smoke.asp.

Singletary, Michelle. "Kick the Tobacco Habit and Stop Sending Your Money Up in Smoke." *Washington Post*, February 1, 2007. http://www.washingtonpost.com/wp-dyn/content/article/2007/01/31/AR2007013101736.html?nav=hcmodule.

Stinson, Robert. "Wayman Manor Fire Accident." *Temple Daily Telegram*, January 10, 2006. http://www.temple-telegram.com/story/2006/01/10/28126.

Tauras, John A., Frank J. Chaloupka, Matthew C. Farrelly, Gary A. Giovino, Melanie Wakefield, Lloyd D. Johnston, Patrick M. O'Malley, Deborah D. Kloska, and Terry F. Pechacek. "State Tobacco Control Spending and Youth Smoking." *American Journal of Public Health* 95 (February 2005): 338–344. http://www.pubmedcentral.nih.gov/articlerender.fcgi?artid=1449175.

U.S. Department of Health and Human Services. *The 2004 Surgeon General's Report, Health Consequences of Smoking: What It Means to You.* Centers for Disease Control and Prevention, National Center for Chronic Disease Prevention and Health Promotion, Office on Smoking and Health, 2004. http://www.cdc.gov/tobacco/data_statistics/sgr/sgr_2004/00_pdfs/SGR2004_Whatitmeanstoyou.pdf.

U.S. Department of Labor Bureau of Labor Statistics. "2002 National Industry-Specific Occupational

Employment and Wage Estimates: NAICS 312200—Tobacco Manufacturing." *Occupational Employment Statistics*, November 26, 2003. http://stat.bls.gov/oes/2002/naics4_312200.htm.

U.S. Fire Administration. "Child Fire Casualties." *Topical Fire Research Series* 1 (March 2001). http://www.usfa.dhs.gov/downloads/pdf/tfrs/v1i17-508.pdf.

Wagner, Susan. *Cigarette Country: Tobacco in American History and Politics.* New York: Praeger Publishers, 1971.

White, Larry C. *Merchants of Death: The American Tobacco Industry.* New York: Beech Tree Books, 1988.

Index

Picture Credits

dreamstime.com
Chupawy: p. 66
Davidcrehner: p. 99
Deserttrends: p. 52
Doctorkan: p. 72
Eperceptions: p. 55
Fintastique: p. 39
Flockholl: p. 56
Icyimage: p. 59
Jeffo: p. 40
Jonoman1: p. 36
Katseyephoto: p. 78
Kenhurst: p. 62
Laurenthamels: p. 71
Loutocky: p. 90
Maxfx: p. 34
Mda: p. 97
Mikeexpert: p. 60
Photodjo: p. 33

Rcmathiraj: p. 76
Rodehi: p. 45

istockphoto.com
Bonzami, Emmanuelle: p. 19
Brosa, Alex: p. 51
Ledbetter, Judy: p. 25
Logan, Dave: p. 15
Popov, Stepan: p. 21

Jupiter Images: p. 13, 22, 26

National Cancer Institute: p. 65

National Institutes of Health: p. 16

To the best knowledge of the publisher, all other images are in the public domain. If any image has been inadvertently uncredited, please notify Harding House Publishing Service, Vestal, New York 13850, so that rectification can be made for future printings.

Author/Consultant Biographies

Author

Amy N. Thomas is a writer and editor whose work has appeared in newsletters and magazines for children. A former middle-school teacher, she now visits classrooms to integrate art and writing with school standards. She became interested in the tobacco industry after losing a relative to emphysema caused by smoking. She has lived and researched in three tobacco-growing states.

Consultant

Wade Berrettini, the consultant for *Smoking: The Dangerous Addiction*, received his MD from Jefferson Medical College and a PhD in Pharmacology from Thomas Jefferson University. For ten years, Dr. Berrettini served as a Fellow at the National Institutes of Health in Bethesda, Maryland, where he studied the genetics of behavioral disorders. Currently Dr. Berrettini is the Karl E. Rickels Professor of Psychiatry and Director, Center for Neurobiology and Behavior at the University of Pennsylvania in Philadelphia. He is also an attending physician at the Hospital of the University of Pennsylvania.

Dr. Berrettini is the author or co-author of more than 250 scientific articles as well as several books. He has conducted ground-breaking genetic research in nicotine addiction. He is the holder of two patents and the recipient of several awards, including recognition by Best Doctors in America 2003–2004, 2005–2006, and 2007–2008.